Library Technology REPORTS

Expert Guides to Library Systems and Services

Learning Management Systems: Tools for Embedded Librarianship

John J. Burke and Beth E. Tumbleson

ALA TechSource
alatechsource.org

American Library Association

Library Technology Reports

ALA TechSource purchases fund advocacy, awareness, and accreditation programs for library professionals worldwide.

Volume 52, Number 2
Learning Management Systems: Tools for Embedded Librarianship
ISBN: 978-0-8389-5970-1

American Library Association
50 East Huron St.
Chicago, IL 60611-2795 USA
alatechsource.org
800-545-2433, ext. 4299
312-944-6780
312-280-5275 (fax)

Advertising Representative
Patrick Hogan
phogan@ala.org
312-280-3240

Editor
Patrick Hogan
phogan@ala.org
312-280-3240

Copy Editor
Judith Lauber

Production
Tim Clifford and Alison Elms

Cover Design
Alejandra Diaz

Library Technology Reports (ISSN 0024-2586) is published eight times a year (January, March, April, June, July, September, October, and December) by American Library Association, 50 E. Huron St., Chicago, IL 60611. It is managed by ALA TechSource, a unit of the publishing department of ALA. Periodical postage paid at Chicago, Illinois, and at additional mailing offices. POSTMASTER: Send address changes to Library Technology Reports, 50 E. Huron St., Chicago, IL 60611.

Trademarked names appear in the text of this journal. Rather than identify or insert a trademark symbol at the appearance of each name, the authors and the American Library Association state that the names are used for editorial purposes exclusively, to the ultimate benefit of the owners of the trademarks. There is absolutely no intention of infringement on the rights of the trademark owners.

ALA TechSource
alatechsource.org

Copyright © 2016
John J. Burke and Beth E. Tumbleson
All Rights Reserved.

About the Authors

John J. Burke is the director of the Gardner-Harvey Library on the Middletown regional campus of Miami University (Ohio) and holds the rank of principal librarian. John is a past president of the Academic Library Association of Ohio and recipient of its Jay Ladd Distinguished Service Award, a former chair of the Library Council of the Southwest Ohio Council on Higher Education and a current board member of OhioNET. He holds an MS in library science from the University of Tennessee and a BA in history from Michigan State University. John has worked in library administration, public services, instruction, collection development, web design, and systems. His scholarship centers on LMS embedded librarianship, makerspaces, and technology for library staff.

Beth E. Tumbleson is assistant director of the Gardner-Harvey Library on the Middletown regional campus of Miami University (Ohio) and holds the rank of associate librarian. She earned her MS in library science from Simmons School of Library Science and an MA in church history from Trinity Evangelical Divinity School. She also earned a BA in English and French from Dickinson College. Beth has worked as an academic, high school, and corporate librarian. She has worked in library administration, distance library services, instruction, and collection development. Her scholarship focuses on LMS embedded librarianship and academic integrity.

Abstract

Learning management system (LMS) embedded librarianship is partnering with faculty to deliver research assistance for students right in their LMS course sites. This issue of *Library Technology Reports* (vol. 52, no. 2), "Learning Management Systems: Tools for Embedded Librarianship," describes the LMS environment alongside the larger online resource environment of academic libraries. Topics include options for adding digital collections and finding tools; methods for creating course-specific content; and online tools for communication, collaboration, and citing sources. The trend of LMS embedded librarians is considered, as well as underlying principles of universal design, instructional design, accessibility, and copyright.

Get Your *Library Technology Reports* Online!

Subscribers to ALA TechSource's *Library Technology Reports* can read digital versions, in PDF and HTML formats, at http://journals.ala.org/ltr. Subscribers also have access to an archive of past issues. After an embargo period of twelve months, *Library Technology Reports* are available open access. The archive goes back to 2001.

Subscriptions

alatechsource.org/subscribe

Contents

Chapter 1—LMS Embedded Librarianship and the Educational Role of Librarians — 5
- LMS Embedded Librarianship — 5
- Responding to Higher Education Development and Challenges — 6
- The LMS Environment — 7
- The LMS Embedded Librarian Opportunity — 8
- Notes — 8

Chapter 2—Digital Collections — 10
- LMS Embedded Librarianship — 10
- Digital Collections — 11
- Full-Text Articles — 11
- E-books — 12
- Dissertations and Theses — 12
- Videos — 13
- Images — 13
- Audio — 13
- Data Sets — 15
- Open Access — 16
- Open Educational Resources — 16
- Notes — 16

Chapter 3—Search Systems and Finding Tools — 17
- LMS Embedded Librarianship — 17
- Index-Based Discovery Services — 17
- Discovery Service — 18
- Databases — 19
- Search Engines — 20
- Portals — 21
- Notes — 21

Chapter 4—Choosing Content-Creation Products — 23
- The LMS Embedded Librarian as a Content Creator — 23
- Course and Subject Guides — 23
- Presentations — 24
- Screencasts — 25
- Interactive Tutorials — 25
- Collections of Instructional Content — 26
- Best Practices for Building Instructional Guides, Presentations, and Tutorials — 26
- Notes — 27

Chapter 5—Communicating, Collaboration, and Citing — 28
- LMS Embedded Librarianship — 28
- Communicating with Students — 28
- LMS Collaboration Tools — 29
- Web Conferencing — 30
- Citation Tools — 32
- Notes — 32

Contents, continued

Chapter 6—Universal Design and Copyright Considerations — **34**

    The Impacts of Universal Design and Copyright on LMS Embedded Librarianship — 34
    Universal Design — 34
    Following Instructional Design Principles — 34
    Accessible Design Considerations — 35
    Responsive Design — 35
    Copyright Considerations in LMS Embedded Librarianship — 35
    Notes — 36

Chapter 1

LMS Embedded Librarianship and the Educational Role of Librarians

LMS Embedded Librarianship

Librarians have long sought new ways to reach out to their users and support those users' research needs. In the age of limited collections of printed materials, libraries drew researchers and readers into their edifices to make use of the library's resources. With the digitization of many materials, librarians now serve a much more physically distributed clientele that uses the library's resources from home and mobile devices as well as in-house. The movement of librarians into learning management systems (LMSs) has been a natural progression as higher education institutions embraced these tools for supporting teaching and learning. Faculty members have gravitated toward using a secure, online means of interacting and sharing course materials with their students, and librarians have followed along to seize new opportunities to market and supply their services.

The larger idea of embedded librarianship was suggested by Barbara Dewey in her 2004 article on library collaboration within institutions.[1] She recommended that librarians become embedded in various forms and facets of university life. Being embedded might involve serving on university or academic department committees, being located in faculty office areas or academic program buildings, or offering library services to university functions like grant seeking and departmental research teams. Embedding has come to be practiced by physically embedding librarians in these ways, but also by creating collaborations between librarians and faculty in the classroom. Librarians assist faculty with research assignment design and guide students in the practices and skills they need to successfully research topics.

Embedding themselves in classes to interact with students about library research corresponds to a larger librarian role as educator. This role is more crucial than ever, as research into first-year college student experiences shows that students are often overwhelmed by the transition to using academic databases.[2] Opportunities to connect with these students who are new to the academic enterprise, as well as with continuing students, increases the chances for students to benefit from the modeling of research practices and to provide feedback on searching choices. Library directors have risen to this challenge, identifying library instruction services as the most important library service function in one national survey.[3] Institutional support for this role is clear, as is the impetus for instruction in information literacy from professional bodies. The newly developed *Framework for Information Literacy for Higher Education* from the Association of College and Research Libraries was intended to provide new approaches for teaching students the essentials of information literacy in collaboration with teaching faculty.[4]

LMS embedded librarianship takes the embedding concept and librarians' educational role into the virtual environment of the LMS. Embedded librarians connect with faculty, who add the librarians to their LMS course sites in both online and face-to-face courses. The librarian then adds links to library resources, screencasts on using databases or working through the steps of research, citation guidance, and more. The librarian becomes a member of the course, with full access to assignments, course materials, discussion forums, and other resources provided by the instructor. This access gives the librarian insights into the course beyond what is typically available when planning a one-shot instruction session. It also provides new opportunities to reveal fitting library resources to students in the context of the course. Embedded librarians now have an avenue to gaining student attention, affixing library resources and librarian guidance to assignment pages and within course modules, and impacting students for the duration of the course through pages of linked resources and participation in class discussions.

Responding to Higher Education Development and Challenges

In addition to the motivations above, LMS embedded librarianship can also address four current trends and challenges in higher education:

- the rise of online learning
- the increasing use of open educational resources (OERs)
- the need to improve digital literacy
- the focus on student success

The Rise of Online Learning

Students continue to choose online learning options in significant numbers. Somewhere between 5.2 million and 7.1 million students were enrolled in at least one distance education course as of 2013, and while the growth rate of online enrollments has slowed, they continue to grow faster than overall higher education enrollments.[5] This count of online students is limited to completely online courses and does not include hybrid or blended courses, which include a significant percentage of online instruction time. Many students are learning in partially or fully online settings or with significant support from online resources.

This fact provides an opportunity for librarians to serve these online students. Bell identified digital education as an increasing revenue source for institutions and a chance for librarians to reach out and support students and faculty.[6] The growing digital nature of the library collection and the inability of online students to visit the library push librarians to become involved. Librarians are no strangers to online communication with users, but such communication has often been limited to questions from individuals and passive provision of resources on library websites. There is no time like the present to become more active in supporting online education. A survey of academic library directors revealed that fewer than 50 percent of them believed that their libraries were prepared to support students online.[7] Another report provided examples of how academic libraries could provide expertise on instructional design for online learning to faculty.[8] The practices that embedded librarians have developed are available for others to adapt, improve, and use.

The Increasing Use of Open Educational Resources (OERs)

Broad concerns about college affordability and a willingness among faculty to share course materials and use the materials of others have driven the creation of open educational resources (OERs) over the past two decades. Repositories of OERs have been created by individual faculty members or associations to share learning objects, including everything from video tutorials and quizzes to textbooks, with their colleagues at no or low cost. "Open" items are generally licensed so that they can be shared with students for free as well, using established systems such as Creative Commons licensing.[9] The aim is to produce high-quality teaching resources that can be shared digitally with a wide audience, possibly saving students from high textbook costs and educators from reinventing the wheel. The LMS provides a structure in which to link or embed OERs for a course.

As faculty members supplement their coursework with freely available, shared educational resources, librarians can play multiple roles in the process. They may serve as locators and gatherers of OER content, helping to connect interested faculty with items that will work within their disciplines, at the right level of study, and with the proper focus for the specific courses.[10] Academic libraries have served as funders and hosts for OER projects, helping to support the efforts of content creators and ensuring that their work will be available over time.[11] Librarians can also supplement digital OER content with articles, e-books, and other licensed database content that can be seamlessly linked from an LMS course site. Embedded librarians can build relationships with faculty that help in all of these aspects of providing OERs, utilizing the searching and collecting skills of an individual who is also knowledgeable about the course content and assignments.

The Need to Improve Digital Literacy

While the definition of *digital literacy* remains in flux, educators at all levels see improvements in students' digital literacy as crucial. The range of elements included in the term include applying technology in educational activities and evaluating digital sources of information. Current approaches to improving digital literacy suggest preparing higher education faculty to assist students in gaining greater skill in using technology, along with including digital literacy in the curriculum.[12] Students would become more comfortable with the various facets of digital literacy, from creating online presentations and videos to choosing appropriate sources for their research from search engine results. The goal would be to make sure that students have the skills to make use of technology now and in the future, in academic coursework and the workplace.

The common connection here for faculty and librarians is that digital literacy overlaps with information literacy, and librarians are used to working in digital environments and using technology. While academic librarians may feel that their institutions have only a passing interest in information literacy, paying attention to it only in connection with accreditation or academic integrity campaigns, there appears to be sustained interest in digital literacy. This is partly due to the fact that as digital tools and practices continue to proliferate and change, there are endless new permutations of digital literacy to discuss.[13] Here again, putting librarians in the midst of an online learning environment allows them to connect with students on questions of digital literacy. The academic library profession is providing new tools for these librarians through the *Framework for Information Literacy*, which should help practitioners communicate literacy concepts to students and faculty alike.[14] The LMS embedded librarian is situated on the front lines of connecting information and digital literacy to course activities, whether or not they are formally adopted into the curriculum.

The Focus on Student Success

Student success, as measured by graduation and retention, is a crucial concern for all institutions. A fundamental motivation is the desire to see all students succeed in earning degrees and meeting their educational goals. A very practical motivation is the need for student tuition dollars, paid by continuing students, to sustain the institution. For public institutions in some states, there is the added motivation of maximizing the amount of state funding the institutions receive by increasing student graduation and retention rates. Educators and administrators are in higher education to see students learn and complete their objectives, and librarians share that aim.

Academic librarians are trying a variety of methods for supporting students and keeping them on track to complete courses and graduate. Many of the instructional efforts practiced by librarians have the underlying goal of making students more successful in their assignments. Now, librarians are trying to quantify the impact they have on students and to find ways to measure their value.[15] Identifying methods of doing so will allow librarians to demonstrate clearly the importance of their involvement with students and to make a case for the best way to implement future programs. Embedded librarians can help this effort by doing what they do well: becoming part of courses, understanding faculty expectations, and collaborating with faculty to impact students at the moments of greatest need for research assistance, An important element of embedded librarianship is that it often offers prolonged opportunities for the librarian to interact with students and to see the growth of their skills over the duration of the course. Also, Bell stated that he expects increased opportunities to use student data to measure student competencies in research and related skills.[16] These learning analytics measures can be and have been easily implemented within an LMS, which once again puts the embedded librarian right at the heart of a key area of measuring student achievement.

The LMS Environment

Increases in online learning and in use of LMSs at institutions for both online and face-to-face courses have made LMS embedded librarianship much more feasible and all the more important for librarians. The combination of online courses, hybrid courses, and face-to-face courses leads to increasing use of LMSs. In a 2014 EDUCAUSE survey, 86 percent of faculty respondents reported using an LMS in at least one of their courses; 83 percent of student respondents in the same survey reported using the campus LMS in at least one of their courses, and 56 percent used the LMS in most or all of their courses.[17] The opportunities are there for embedded librarians to reach students and impact their research success.

The LMS market contains a number of major companies. The largest LMS companies in the United States in terms of numbers of institutions served are (in order) Blackboard, Moodle, Canvas, BrightSpace (D2L), and Sakai. There has been much merger and acquisition activity in the market over time, with Blackboard taking on a number of other systems and maintaining a dominant presence. Blackboard currently has a 33.5 percent share of US institutions, not including installations of Angel, a formerly independent LMS that Blackboard still offers under its own name. Canvas is currently growing fastest, with a 40 percent increase in installations between 2013 and 2014, while the other players have remained stable.[18]

Tumbleson and Burke's survey of embedded librarians also found that the companies discussed above, in general, were the dominant LMS vendors.[19] The notable exception was Canvas, which had only a small number of installations at that time. It is good to be aware of the other players in the market, beyond the one currently used at a given institution, as universities and colleges are prone to change systems, driven largely by economics and user experience. The authors' institution, for example, is now on its third LMS since 2009. Generally, the library will have little input into the choice of an LMS, and librarians will need to become familiar with the platform that is available.

Largest LMS Companies

Blackboard
www.blackboard.com

Moodle
https://moodle.org

Canvas
www.canvaslms.com

BrightSpace (D2L)
www.brightspace.com

Sakai
https://sakaiproject.org

All LMSs, regardless of platform, provide a set of common features and capabilities for students, faculty, and librarians. The following items can be utilized by librarians to reach students and share important content:

- **Content pages** can be posted in the course site, whether produced within the LMS content editor interface or created outside as HTML, PDF, or other types of files. This allows the embedded librarian to post a page listing contact information for the librarian, links to useful resources, tutorials, and step-by-step guidance on searching. It also lets the librarian, with permission from the instructor, add specific library resources or links to the larger resource page to other course documents, such as assignments, specific lessons or modules, or the syllabus.
- **E-mailing** students who are enrolled in the course is easy with a built-in e-mail interface. It is often difficult for librarians to communicate with students beyond face-to-face instruction time. The LMS environment allows the librarian to introduce herself to students and have opportunities to remind students of her presence later in the semester or quarter.
- **Discussion boards or forums** are often used by faculty members to provide students a venue to ask questions and to hold discussions of class materials and topics. Some embedded librarians will set up a separate "ask the librarian" board or forum for students' research questions. Other librarians may monitor a general class discussion board, perhaps participating only during times preceding research project due dates. The board or forum offers an opportunity to respond to individuals' questions in a group format so that the entire class can benefit from the responses. It is also a place to post tips or highlight resources away from the embedded librarian resources page.
- **Web conferencing tools** are provided for synchronous interaction with individuals, groups, or the entire class, perhaps involving just chat exchanges, but more likely involving shared video information as well. They can be used for appointment-based research consultation meetings with students in which the librarian demonstrates useful databases and suggests directions for research to take. They could also serve as the location of an online version of a face-to-face instruction session for an entire class.

The LMS Embedded Librarian Opportunity

Librarians have a great opportunity before them to reach out to students and collaborate with faculty. Embedded librarianship in the LMS builds on librarians' abilities and provision of technology and instructional support to students and faculty. The expertise that librarians continue to grow in instructional design, open educational resources, copyright, and digital learning objects can be brought together in successful partnerships that positively impact students. The material shared in the coming chapters will explore resources and finding tools to link to in the LMS and ways to use the LMS to communicate with students. In addition, there will be a discussion of how to design the LMS embedded presence and technologies to use to organize and convey information that students need.

Notes

1. Barbara I. Dewey, "The Embedded Librarian: Strategic Campus Collaborations," *Resource Sharing and Information Networks* 17, no. 1–2 (2014): 5–17, http://dx.doi.org/10.1300/J121v17n01_02.
2. Alison J. Head, *Learning the Ropes: How Freshmen Conduct Course Research Once They Enter College*, Project Information Literacy Research Report: The Passage Studies (Seattle: University of Washington Information School, December 5, 2013), http://projectinfolit.org/images/pdfs/pil_2013_freshmen study_fullreport.pdf.
3. Matthew P. Long and Roger C. Schonfeld, *Ithaka S+R US Library Survey 2013* (New York: Ithaka, March 11,

2014), 14–15, http://sr.ithaka.org?p=22787.
4. Association of College and Research Libraries, *Framework for Information Literacy for Higher Education*, ACRL MW15 Doc 4.1 (Chicago: Association of College and Research Libraries, January 2015), http://acrl.ala.org/ilstandards/wp-content/uploads/2015/01/Framework-MW15-Board-Docs.pdf.
5. I. Elaine Allen and Jeff Seaman, *Grade Level: Tracking Online Education in the United States*, research report (Oakland, CA: Babson Survey Research Group and Quahog Research Group, February 2015), 5, www.onlinelearningsurvey.com/reports/gradelevel.pdf.
6. Steven Bell, "Top 10 Academic Library Issues for 2015," From the Bell Tower, *Library Journal*, February 18, 2015, http://lj.libraryjournal.com/2015/02/opinion/steven-bell/top-10-academic-library-issues-for-2015-from-the-bell-tower.
7. Long and Schonfeld, *Ithaka S+R US Library Survey*, 34–35.
8. Larry Johnson, Samantha Adams Becker, Victoria Estrada, and Alex Freeman, *NMC Horizon Report: 2015 Library Edition* (Austin, TX: New Media Consortium, 2015), 28, http://cdn.nmc.org/media/2015-nmc-horizon-report-library-EN.pdf.
9. Larry Johnson, Samantha Adams Becker, Victoria Estrada, and Alex Freeman, *NMC Horizon Report: 2015 Higher Education Edition* (Austin, TX: New Media Consortium, 2015), 14–15, http://cdn.nmc.org/media/2015-nmc-horizon-report-HE-EN.pdf.
10. Bell, "Top 10 Academic Library Issues."
11. ACRL Research Planning and Review Committee, "Top Trends in Academic Libraries: A Review of the Trends and Issues Affecting Academic Libraries in Higher Education," *College and Research Libraries News* 75, no. 6 (June 2014): 296–97, http://crln.acrl.org/content/75/6/294.full.
12. Johnson et al., *NMC Horizon Report: 2015 Higher Education Edition*, 24–25.
13. Johnson et al., *NMC Horizon Report: 2015 Library Edition*, 24–25.
14. Association of College and Research Libraries, *Framework for Information Literacy*.
15. ACRL Research Planning and Review Committee, "Top Trends in Academic Libraries," 297–98.
16. Bell, "Top 10 Academic Library Issues."
17. Eden Dahlstrom and Jacqueline Bichsel, *ECAR Study of Undergraduate Students and Information Technology, 2014*, research report (Louisville, CO: EDUCAUSE Center for Analysis and Research, October 2014), 10, https://net.educause.edu/ir/library/pdf/ss14/ERS1406.pdf.
18. Phil Hill, "State of the US Higher Education LMS Market: 2014 Edition," *e-Literate* (blog), October 22, 2014, http://mfeldstein.com/state-us-higher-education-lms-market-2014-edition.
19. Beth E. Tumbleson and John J. Burke, *Embedding Librarianship in Learning Management Systems* (Chicago: ALA/Neal-Schuman, 2013), 147.

Chapter 2

Digital Collections

LMS Embedded Librarianship

LMS embedded librarians are engaged in student learning according to the Ithaka S+R US Library Survey 2013. They confer with faculty members to discover what their learning outcomes are and what their research assignments entail. After considering what students will have to know and do as researchers, the librarian identifies which subject databases are most appropriate. Academic libraries will license and sometimes buy hundreds of these subject databases. In addition to this proprietary content, LMS embedded librarians guide students to open-access content and open educational resources freely available online. Knowledge of the subject discipline, the library's collections, and the changing publishing landscape is needed to list and link to the best digital collections available for students. Often the LMS embedded librarian will create or link to available tutorials in an effort to explain visually how to navigate search interfaces and how the various collections overlap or are distinct from one another. With this kind of support, students are better able to decide which digital collections are most suited to their research needs.

The LMS embedded librarian might work in the following manner. After discussing the details of a research project with a professor, the librarian begins to build an LMS embedded librarian page or a course LibGuide for registered students. This is a carefully selected resource list, drawn from all digital collections available through the university libraries and online. After linking to general contact information, the embedded librarian may recommend databases that suggest topic ideas on controversial issues in the news, such as EBSCO's Points of View Reference Center or Gale's Opposing Viewpoints in Context or CQ Researcher. Individual electronic reference titles published by various companies (Gale, Oxford, Salem, Springer, Wiley, etc.) or reference collections like Credo can also be linked to for academic background research. The librarian proceeds to link to the library discovery service for its digital and print collections. The comprehensive discovery service for articles, books, and media may be highlighted using tutorials that demonstrate its purpose and search interface. Several subject databases may be individually linked to promote essential digital collections within a field, such as images in Artstor for art; scholarly journal articles in Criminal Justice Abstracts with Full Text for criminal justice; evidence-based practice reviews in the Cochrane Library for nursing; or company and market data in OneSource for business. Sometimes the LMS embedded librarian will need to steer students to specialized digital collections in statistics—like the Statistical Abstract of the United States by ProQuest or American FactFinder by the US Census Bureau—or in law—like LexisNexis for legal cases.

Normally the embedded librarian will include screencasts or screenshots that demonstrate how to conduct efficient online searching, explain research terminology such as *peer-reviewed*, describe a discipline-specific thesaurus such as the National Library of Medicine's Medical Subject Headings (MeSH) or codes used in business research such as the North American Industry Classification System (NAICS), or introduce a mnemonic system for evaluating websites such as the CRAAP Test: Currency, Relevance, Authority, Accuracy, Purpose. Finally, the embedded librarian will link to guides, generators, and managers for the required citation style or styles students will use. By carefully directing students to these academic tools, explaining research concepts, and linking to digital collections, the LMS embedded librarian is able to help students develop their information literacy and encourage them to adopt more productive research strategies based upon a fuller understanding of the cycle of scholarly communication.

Digital Collections

Embedded librarians have many choices when it comes to directing students to scholarly digital collections within their LMS courses. Today, most academic libraries license or buy digital collections such as databases of full-text articles, dissertations, images, music, and videos as well as electronic journals and books. "Since 1995 our function has been, increasingly, to secure for our patrons the collective right to access and use digital documents that are housed and cared for elsewhere."[1] Academic libraries are transitioning from local print collections to remotely accessible, online collections, in part to reduce storage costs for print, which can be housed in high-density storage off site or replaced entirely by digital collections. User space for creation and collaboration has become a greater priority than collection storage in the physical library in higher education. This trend in collection development has been well documented by leaders in library and information science in various reports and studies (*NMC Horizon Report*: 2015 Library Edition, and David Lewis's 2013 *College and Research Libraries* article). Among librarians and scholars, this move towards greater reliance on digital collections and renovated, repurposed library space has been neither tranquil nor uncontested. Indeed, city-wide debates and litigation regarding the New York Public Library illustrates the discord such facilities decisions may unleash.[2]

Today's readers value instant access to content on their mobile devices. According to a 2014 report by the EDUCAUSE Center for Analysis Research, 60 percent of students access library resources via mobile devices.[3] While some view digital content online, others choose to download it and read it offline later. Views and downloads have become the new metrics library administrators study. Students and researchers in higher education increasingly expect online, full-text access to documents. Digital content is available for all learning styles. These digital documents have the advantage of immediate access from anywhere and can be marked up and shared with colleagues. According to the *NMC Horizon Report*, users prefer web-scale discovery of items, linked to library holdings of their institution.[4] In short, scholarship has gone digital and is headed towards open access. This priority expands the possibility of access to global scholarship over local physical collection development. Users understand and desire the ideal of simultaneous, unlimited, free access to information, thus ensuring equitable global access; however, it is not yet a reality.

Full-Text Articles

Anyone who attends national conferences and has strolled the exhibition hall is familiar with the major publishers that create and maintain databases of full-text articles. EBSCOhost, Elsevier, Gale, LexisNexis, ProQuest, and Thomson Reuters provide electronic access to current and back files of scholarly journals, popular magazines, and newspapers. Today's academic libraries are most likely to provide access to these full-text databases through subscriptions, licensing, or consortia-shared licensing. Publishers may opt to sell access to articles through full-text databases, through subscriptions to their journal titles, or even through access to individual articles. Pricing varies, depending on terms such as site license, building or location license, full-time equivalent (FTE) ranges, consortial multipliers from one to unlimited, simultaneous access, the number of units the institution already pays to that publisher, and timing due to special deals at the end of the quarter or the year. Clearly, pricing models are somewhat mysterious and require experienced negotiators' advocacy and action as vendors rethink their cash-flow models and reorganize their operations and adjust their pricing accordingly.

Not only are current journals available electronically, so too are historical journals and newspapers. Readex, a division of NewsBank Inc., offers three centuries under the label "America's Historical Newspapers," including "America's Early Newspapers Series 1–7, 1690–1922" (www.readex.com). JSTOR provides access to archival collections I–XI of scholarly journals in all disciplines (www.jstor.org).

Other traditional approaches to access are used as well. Document delivery services are made available by academic libraries to their users as an economical solution for providing quick access to a particular article. While an annual serial subscription may strain a library budget, paying for one specific article retains the user's goodwill and remains affordable for libraries. Libraries also provide interlibrary loan services to supply needed full-text articles at no cost to the user, while the library absorbs the expenses of staff time and associated fees. Sometimes users will find the desired article in an institutional repository or scholarly commons in the form of a preprint, postprint, or publisher's version or PDF. Some institutions require faculty and staff to upload their articles to make them freely available, while

> **Full-Text Solutions**
> - document delivery services
> - institutional repositories
> - interlibrary loan services
> - statewide or regional library consortia

others leave it to the personal choice of the faculty or staff member. It is apparent that access to full-text articles can be no cost, low cost, or quite costly, depending on the suppliers' terms. Rarely is there a one-price-fits-all model.

E-books

More e-books are becoming available through libraries as publishers explore various business models. Libraries are able to acquire e-book collections from publishers and aggregators that build discipline-specific collections, such as nursing, and thematic collections, such as reference. In addition to buying or licensing e-book collections, it is also possible to order individual titles from publishers, even from major publishers like Oxford University Press, which had resisted allowing this option, through the academic book jobber, Yankee Book Peddler (YBP). Publishers are moving toward releasing more e-books simultaneously with their print editions. Frontlist e-book titles are becoming more readily available for libraries to order. Publishers that preferred to sell e-book versions of only backlisted, older titles are now willing to sell to libraries both electronic and print editions of newly released monographs.

Library pricing models for e-books are still under debate, however. Readers will recall the arbitrary limit of twenty-six loans per year implemented by Harper-Collins. Librarians recognize that library prices are much higher than what the individual reader may pay for the same e-book. Another consideration is multiplier costs for a given number of simultaneous users within an institution or a consortium. Prices must be thoughtfully negotiated. A workable solution for electronic book interlibrary loans among libraries has yet to be achieved, although interlibrary loan e-book pilots have been run, like the Occam's Reader Project (http://occamsreader.org).

Another complicating aspect of electronic books concerns the e-book readers, or e-readers, necessary to read digital content. There are various open and proprietary e-book formats in use, such as PDF and EPUB, which present format compatibility issues to be considered with commercial e-readers. Apps can be used to read an e-book online or offline, on a desktop, laptop, tablet, or smartphone. Check the device's operating system. Determine whether it will be necessary to buy or borrow dedicated hardware such as a Barnes and Noble Nook or Amazon Kindle. Find out if it is necessary to download special software such as Adobe Digital Editions or if the e-reader is browser-based, as is true of the new EBSCO online e-book viewer. EBSCO (https://www.ebscohost.com/ebooks) offers a collection of more than 15,000 e-books. Is the e-book device-neutral? Can library users avoid becoming enmeshed in confusing digital rights management (DRM) difficulties?

There are many e-book database collections, which can be broad in scope or quite focused: Digitalia Hispanica (Latin American and Spanish literature, https://www.amigos.org/node/2665), R2 Digital Library (nursing, www.r2library.com), National Academies Press (STEM titles, www.nap.edu), Project MUSE (books and journals in the humanities and social sciences, https://muse.jhu.edu), Safari Online (technology, https://www.safaribooksonline.com), Salem Press (reference titles, www.salempress.com), Wiley Online Library (multi-disciplinary books and journals), and Stalin Digital Archive (digital primary sources). This list indicates the range of disciplines and genres covered in e-books. In addition, individual in-print e-book titles can be selected from Amazon or the academic book jobber Yankee Book Peddler, recently acquired by EBSCO. Not only newly published titles, but also historical books are being distributed as e-books. Three centuries of individual historical texts can be accessed via Readex's America's Historical Imprints (www.readex.com/content/americas-historical-imprints): Early American Imprints, Series I: Evans, 1639–1800, ProQuest's Early English Books Online (www.proquest.com/products-services/databases/eebo.html), and Gale Cengage Learning's Eighteenth Century Collections Online (http://gale.cengage.co.uk/product-highlights/history/eighteenth-century-collections-online.aspx). SAGE Knowledge (https://us.sagepub.com/en-us/nam/knowledge) has been publishing its Historic Documents series of primary sources since 1972.

Dissertations and Theses

ProQuest/UMI indexes doctoral dissertations and master's theses from more than seven hundred universities. Its extensive archive is worldwide, beginning in 1743; the first American dissertation dates from 1861. Each year ProQuest archives more than ninety thousand new graduate works, which it then disseminates. Libraries subscribe to ProQuest's Dissertation and Theses bibliographic database of abstracts so that students, authors, researchers, and publishing institutions may search for, identify, and access graduate works of interest. The dissertations and theses may be purchased or downloaded for a fee, but it is often possible to borrow them through interlibrary loan services for free (www.proquest.com/products-services/dissertations).

Videos

Many students satisfy their personal preference for visual learning by watching digital videos. In addition, faculty assign digital videos or clips as part of regular classroom instruction. Sometimes students view a video together in class, and sometimes individually outside class as homework. Digital videos or clips can be linked or embedded in learning management courses and streamed. Some commercial vendors allow subscribers to search across multiple video collections simultaneously, for example, Alexander Street Press, which offers this functionality in its Academic Video Online platform. Other commercial vendors, such as Kanopy, Kaltura, and Films on Demand (by Films Media Group), offer streaming of clips and complete videos. Still other vendors, such as Lynda.com and Atomic Learning, offer video training in technology and software applications as well as academic concepts. Commercial news databases, like AP Archive and NBC Learn, offer archives of news videos from the 1920s to the present. Scholastic BookFlix includes PreK–3 storybook and nonfiction videos to strengthen a love of reading and literacy. In addition, free digital videos may be located at YouTube, TED Talks, and Kahn Academy, where users may learn and review core subjects.

Free Video Search Tools

Blinkx
www.blinkx.com

ClipBlast!
www.clipblast.com

Creative Commons Search
https://search.creativecommons.org

Google Videos
https://www.google.com/videohp

OVGuide
https://www.ovguide.com

Tenplay
http://tenplay.com.au

Images

Images, maps, and photographs accent the visual and clarify textual descriptions and explanations. Professors and presenters may include images in class lectures, syllabi, and research findings to inspire the imagination, add humor, or clarify concepts. Images can be found both through commercial producers like Artstor (art and architecture images), Images of the American Civil War by Alexander Street Press, JSTOR Global Plants, or iStock by Getty Images.

Free Image Suppliers

American Memory (Library of Congress)
http://memory.loc.gov/ammem/index.html

Digital Public Library of America
http://dp.la

Flickr
https://www.flickr.com

Google Images
https://images.google.com

Wikipedia Commons
https://commons.wikimedia.org/wiki/Main_Page

Audio

Podcasts and music contribute to the learning experience. Some collections are free, such as the Library of Congress's American Memory, which includes oral histories and sound recordings. Other free sources include SoundCloud (https://soundcloud.com), the world's leading social sound platform using apps that allow users to upload, record, promote, and share original audio creations; Jamendo Music (https://www.jamendo.com/?language=en), a free service for digital music that also offers a music licensing platform; ccMixter (http://ccmixter.org), which allows downloads, listening, and remixes, with its community making mashups, remixes, and a cappella tracks under Creative Commons licenses. In addition, National Jukebox (www.loc.gov/jukebox/) provides historical recordings from the Library of Congress. Podcasts from radio broadcasts are included in proprietary databases like Gale's Opposing Viewpoints in Context (http://solutions.cengage.com/InContext/Opposing-Viewpoints/). Proprietary music databases like American Song (http://alexanderstreet.com/products/american-song), Naxos Music Library (https://www.naxosmusiclibrary.com/home.asp?rurl=%2Fdefault%2Easp), and Smithsonian

Digital Content Providers

Database Vendors

EBSCOhost
https://www.ebscohost.com

Gale
www.cengage.com/us

LexisNexis
www.lexisnexis.com/en-us/gateway.page

ProQuest
www.proquest.com

Thomson Reuters
http://thomsonreuters.com/en.html

Electronic Journals

Elsevier
www.elsevier.com

SAGE Publications
https://us.sagepub.com/en-us/nam/home

Springer
www.springer.com/us

Wiley
www.wiley.com/WileyCDA

Directory of Open Access Journals
https://doaj.org

E-books

ABC-CLIO
www.abc-clio.com

Cambridge University Press
www.cambridge.org

ebrary
www.ebrary.com/corp

EBSCOhost
https://www.ebscohost.com

Gale Virtual Reference Library
www.cengage.com/search/showresults.do?N=197+4294904997

JSTOR
www.jstor.org

Oxford Scholarship Online
www.oxfordscholarship.com

Project MUSE
https://muse.jhu.edu

Safari Books Online
www.proquest.com/products-services/safari_tech_books.html

SAGE Publications
https://us.sagepub.com/en-us/nam/home

Salem Press
www.salempress.com

Springer
www.springer.com/us

Wiley
www.wiley.com/WileyCDA

Open-Access E-books

Directory of Open Access Books
https://doabooks.org

Google Books
https://books.google.com

Project Gutenberg
https://archive.org/details/gutenberg

HathiTrust Digital Library
https://www.hathitrust.org

E-book Comparisons

Comparison of e-book formats
https://en.wikipedia.org/wiki/Comparison_of_e-book_formats

Comparison of e-book readers
https://en.wikipedia.org/wiki/Comparison_of_e-book_readers

Dissertations

Dissertations and Theses Dissemination and Ordering (ProQuest)
www.proquest.com/products-services/dissertations

Open Access Dissertations and Theses
https://oatd.org

PQDT Open
http://pqdtopen.proquest.com/search.html

Commercial Videos

Alexander Street
http://alexanderstreet.com

JoVE (Journal of Visualized Experiments)
www.jove.com

Kanopy
https://www.kanopystreaming.com

Free Videos

Kahn Academy
https://www.khanacademy.org

TED Talks
https://www.ted.com

YouTube
https://www.youtube.com

Commercial Images

AP Images
www.apimages.com

Artstor
www.artstor.org

Free Images

Flickr
https://www.flickr.com

Google Images
https://images.google.com

Commercial Audio Resources

American Song
http://alexanderstreet.com/products/american-song

Naxos Music Library
https://www.naxosmusiclibrary.com/home.asp?rurl=%2Fdefault%2Easp

Jazz Music Library
http://alexanderstreet.com/products/jazz-music-library

Smithsonian Global Sound for Libraries
http://alexanderstreet.com/products/smithsonian-global-sound%C2%AE-libraries

Free Audio Resources

Audio Recordings (Library of Congress)
www.loc.gov/audio/collections

National Jukebox (Library of Congress)
www.loc.gov/jukebox

National Public Radio (under programs & podcasts)
www.npr.org

Open Access Resources

arXiv
http://arxiv.org

PLOS (Public Library of Science)
https://www.plos.org

Open Knowledge Repository (World Bank)
https://openknowledge.worldbank.org

Commercial Learning Resources

Atomic Learning
https://www.atomiclearning.com

LearningExpress Library
www.learningexpresshub.com/productengine/LELIndex.html#/learningexpresslibrary/libraryhome

Lynda
www.lynda.com

Commercial Data

SimplyMap
https://www.simplymap.com/login.html

ProQuest Statistical Abstract of the United States
www.proquest.com/products-services/statabstract.html

Wharton Research Data Services (WRDS)
www.whartonwrds.com

Free Data

American FactFinder
http://factfinder.census.gov/faces/nav/jsf/pages/index.xhtml

Data.gov
www.data.gov

Open Educational Resources (OERs)

John Burke, Textbook Alternatives & OER, Miami University Libraries
http://libguides.lib.miamioh.edu/textbookalternatives

Global Sound (http://alexanderstreet.com/products/smithsonian-global-sound%C2%AE-libraries) introduce listeners to their musical heritage and history. It is also possible to learn seventy foreign languages, including ancient languages, by taking advantage of the audio and video files in Mango Languages (https://www.mangolanguages.com).

Data Sets

Digital content is available in proprietary databases—for example, Key Business Ratios, Historical Statistics of the United States, Statistical Abstracts of the United States, and SimplyMap—as well as in free collections like American FactFinder, Business and Industry Statistics by the US Census Bureau, Census Reporter, Centers for Disease Control and Prevention, Data.gov, National Center for Education Statistics, Organization for Co-operation and Development (OECD), UNdata, World Bank's Data and Research, International Monetary Fund Data, and NationMaster for country comparisons.

Open Access

The open-access movement began in the late 1990s and promotes unrestricted access to scholarly research online. Open-access may be *gratis* (free of charge), or it may be *libre*, which means free of charge with some additional usage restrictions, as with Creative Commons licenses. Authors may self-archive their articles in a repository, which is referred to as *green open access*, or publish in an open-access journal, which is known as *gold open access*.

ArXiv.org is an open-access repository of more than a half million scholarly electronic articles in the sciences maintained by Cornell University Library. Cornell University Vision and Image Analysis Group provides publically accessible and available medical image databases. Finding tools for open-access collections include the Directory of Open Access Books (www.doabooks.org), maintained by the OAPEN Foundation at the National Library in the Hague, and the Directory of Open Access Journals (https://doaj.org), founded at Lund University, Sweden, which includes 10,000 open-access scholarly journals in all disciplines.

Open Educational Resources

The term *open educational resources* refers to content for learning, teaching, and research that remains in the public domain and is freely accessible for use and repurposing. These resources may include open textbooks and openly licensed videos, software, learning objects, courses, and tests.

Please note: The commercial and free suppliers listed in the gray boxes serve as an indicative listing rather than a comprehensive list.

Notes

1. Rick Anderson, "A Quiet Culture War in Research Libraries—and What It Means for Librarians, Researchers and Publishers," *Insights* 28, no. 2 (July 2015): 22, Library, Information Science & Technology Abstracts with Full Text, EBSCOhost, http://dx.doi.org/10.1629/uksg.230.
2. Scott Sherman, "The New York Public Library Wars: What Went Wrong at One of the World's Eminent Research Institutions?" *Chronicle of Higher Education* 61, no. 40 (June 24, 2015): B9–B11, Academic Search Complete, EBSCOhost, http://chronicle.com/article/The-New-York-Public-Library/231127.
3. Eden Dahlstrom and Jacqueline Bichsel, *ECAR Study of Undergraduate Students and Information Technology, 2014*, research report (Louisville, CO: EDUCAUSE Center for Analysis and Research, October 2014), 21–22, https://net.educause.edu/ir/library/pdf/ss14/ERS1406.pdf.
4. Larry Johnson, Samantha Becker, Victoria Estrada, and Alex Freeman, *NMC Horizon Report: 2014 Higher Education Edition* (Austin, TX: New Media Consortium, 2014), 14, www.editlib.org/p/130341.

Chapter 3

Search Systems and Finding Tools

LMS Embedded Librarianship

Academic libraries rely on diverse search systems and finding tools. Web-scale discovery platforms have become the preferred search and have replaced federated searching, which was seen as slow and "too cumbersome to serve our students well."[1] Users value an intuitive, simple, and comprehensive search experience. Accordingly, librarians today are reviewing and licensing the next-generation catalog and other discovery tools, often referred to as a discovery layer, discovery service, or discovery user interface. If college and university libraries decide to utilize a truly comprehensive discovery service, then their other traditional tools become less important for searching. Often the work of LMS embedded librarianship includes introducing users to the new discovery service and clarifying what material types and formats are being searched in order that users do not overlook significant resources. Wrong assumptions and incomplete findings can result if these details are unclear.

The LMS embedded librarian minimizes researchers' frustration, confusion, and time when she explains where to start searching and why, as well as what each finding tool is intended to discover. Many administrative decisions about the operation of a discovery system are made locally, and these decisions affect how different types of materials are discovered by searchers, so it becomes imperative for the LMS embedded librarian to offer a recommended order of search with rationale. For example, some academic libraries may set up their discovery service to identify books, articles, institutional repository items, and open-access content in one search. Administrators of another library's discovery service may separate the next-generation catalog for books, e-books, institutional repository items, and open-access content from its discovery service for articles. So if a student is searching for articles on a given topic, it makes sense to start with the library's discovery service for articles, which would incorporate many databases. If a student wants a medical e-book, then using the library's discovery service for books is the logical beginning. At other times, the researcher may prefer the sophisticated search interface of a single database and start with databases A–Z to locate that database. A student who wants information from online news or an individual's website will start with a search engine. A researcher who needs carefully selected, discipline-specific websites may start searching from a portal such as the Virtual Religion Index. In short, need drives the selection of which finding tool is most appropriate because the tools differ and do not discover the same sources. As much as students may like the convenience and ease of starting with Google, that search engine does not do it all.

Index-Based Discovery Services

Next-generation catalogs are turning to discovery. The most significant criterion for a discovery service is its ability to retrieve all library resources in one search, including books, e-books, articles from databases, videos, and items in digital repositories. Often this mechanism relies on a unified index or real-time searching. So the first question to ask is, what is the size of the discovery service's unified index and the extent of coverage of the library's holdings? Admittedly, no discovery service, or search engine for that matter, delivers 100 percent of all resources, so comprehensive finding tools are not a reality yet. The second question to

Leading Discovery Services

EBSCO Discovery Service (EBSCO)
www.ebscohost.com/discovery

Encore Discovery Solution (Innovative Interfaces)
www.iii.com/products/sierra/encore

Primo (Ex Libris)
www.exlibrisgroup.com/category/PrimoOverview

Summon (ProQuest)
www.proquest.com/libraries/academic/discovery-services/

Worldcat Local (OCLC)
www.oclc.org/worldcat-local.en.html

Proprietary Discovery Services

EBSCO Discovery Service (EBSCO)
https://www.ebscohost.com/discovery

Encore Discovery Solution (Innovative Interfaces)
https://www.iii.com/products/sierra/encore

Primo (Ex Libris)
www.exlibrisgroup.com/category/PrimoOverview

Summon (ProQuest)
www.proquest.com/libraries/academic/discovery-services

WorldCat Local (OCLC)
www.oclc.org/worldcat-local.en.html

AquaBrowser (ProQuest)
www.proquest.com/products-services/AquaBrowser.html

Axiell Arena (Axiell)
www.axiell.co.uk/solutions/interface

BiblioCore (BiblioCommons)
www.bibliocommons.com/products/bibliocore

Endeca (Oracle)
www.oracle.com/us/solutions/business-analytics/business-intelligence/endeca/overview/index.html

Enterprise (SirsiDynix)
www.sirsidynix.com/products/enterprise

Visualizer (VTLS)
http://vtls.wikispaces.com

Open-Source Discovery

Blacklight
http://projectblacklight.org

eXtensible Catalog
www.extensiblecatalog.org

VuFind
http://vufind-org.github.io/vufind

pose is, what is the quality of the unified index? How well does it retrieve items from the local institutional repository as well as e-books or patents from the open web?[2] Faceted navigation is expected by searchers as a limiting feature. Relevancy ranking is standard; however, Primo alone offers popularity ranking based on views or usage. Primo alone suggests similar articles. RSS feeds are a nice feature for researchers wishing to be alerted to new materials that match their interests. It is possible to share resources through social networking sites integrated in the discovery service; the majority of products make this possible. A minority of discovery tools offer a persistent link; both EBSCO Discovery Service and WorldCat Local do. The majority of discovery tools supply a separate mobile interface. FRBR enables searchers to find various editions and formats of a work, but this is not a standard feature of most discovery services. Primo and WorldCat Local do offer this desired option. For further details see the excellent review article by Chickering and Yang, which rates Primo and WorldCat Local as the highest scoring discovery tools.[3] Clearly the four vendors of index-based discovery services are competing. Currently, EBSCO "holds the dominant market share, challenged by Ex Libris Primo, OCLE WorldCat Discovery Service, and ProQuest Summon."[4] In October 2015, ProQuest announced it will acquire Ex Libris Group.

Discovery Service

Discovery search systems are replacing federated searching. Discovery systems improve user experience by giving searchers a single starting point to identify all items in the library's holdings. Simple, intuitive, fast searching of everything at once is expected by today's users. "The need to improve user experience was the trigger for the development and deployment of discovery systems and has become the cornerstone of these systems."[5] They enable users to search the library's collections and beyond, note relevancy-ranked items, and get instant access to full text, thus saving the searcher's time. The essential appeal of web-scale discovery is the ease of identifying library materials from publishers, aggregators, and repositories regardless of format or location. They are fast and comprehensive and offer a single search box, familiar to searchers who use Google, the standout among search engines. Libraries wishing to promote their numerous electronic resources are licensing a discovery service so the campus community may conveniently search nearly all holdings simultaneously. Library administrators at last have a means of collecting anonymous

Sixteen Evaluation Criteria for Next-Generation Catalogs

Does the discovery service offer:

- One-stop search?
- A modern web interface?
- Enriched content?
- Faceted navigation?
- A simple keyword search box with a link to advanced search on start page?
- A simple keyword search box on every page?
- Relevancy ranking of results?
- Spelling suggestions?
- Recommend other similar titles?
- An opportunity for user contributions?
- RSS feeds?
- Integration of social networking sites?
- Persistent links?
- Auto-completion/stemming?
- Support for mobile devices?
- Functional Requirements for Bibliographic Retrieval (FRBR)?

Source: F. William Chickering and Sharon Q. Yang, "Evaluation and Comparison of Discovery Tools: An Update," *Information Technology and Libraries* 33, no. 2 (2014): 12–13, Professional Development Collection, EBSCOhost, http://dx.doi.org/10.6017/ital.v33i2.3471.

The main problem here is that students, lacking deep content knowledge, are unlikely to choose well even if they know the best criteria to use and are well motivated. Sadly, for the majority of students, neither knowledge of criteria nor motivation to spend time evaluating is a prominent factor in their research.

Source: William B. Badke, "Expertise and Authority in an Age of Crowdsourcing," in *Not Just Where to Click: Teaching Students How to Think About Information*, Publications in Librarianship no. 68, edited by Troy A. Swanson and Heather Jagman, (Chicago: American Library Association, 2015), 205.

usage data for assessment. With advances in technology, scholars now have access to discovery systems with their increasingly personalized options that facilitate research. Undergraduate searchers who lack expertise have one starting discovery tool that allows them to apply facets to the many results returned to reduce irrelevant hits. Facets may include availability, format, publication year, journal name, database, language, and so on. Although academic libraries are making sizeable investments in updating their search tools, not all librarians enthusiastically support the transition to discovery services. Some librarians have reservations concerning relevancy rankings, evaluation, and authority for reasons that follow.

Academic research continues to challenge students. First, there is the problem of too much information. Although discovery search systems offer limiting features, students tend not to use them. Students turn to trial-and-error keyword searching. According to Asher, "By relying so heavily on simple keyword searches while simultaneously failing to use features to narrow down or refine search results, students were regularly working with an overabundance of search results and potential resources."[6] When searchers are confronted with too many results, they solve this problem via relevancy rankings. Relevancy ranking is problematic, says Asher, who reports undergraduates place too much trust in discovery systems' proprietary algorithms while failing to evaluate sources for themselves. Students' choice of source type is impacted by the search tool they use. The Discovery Tools Project revealed that the biases of the search tools (Google Scholar, Summon, EDS, Library Catalog/Databases, No Tool) influenced the source types students chose—academic journal articles, books, newspapers/magazines/trade journals, for-pay articles, websites, government documents, and other documents.[7]

Because students are hard-pressed to evaluate scholarly sources without "deep content knowledge," they rely on the convenience of relevancy rankings.[8] Typically, students review only the first page of results. Nor do students spend sufficient time and thought working with sources, which presents further problems. According to the Citation Project, three quarters of all student citations involve the first three pages of a source, whatever its length.[9] Obviously, reliance on the introductory source pages skews students' research understanding of academic issues. Instruction in digital literacy as discussed in chapter 1, as well as information literacy, are crucial for student researchers. Both should be added to the course curriculum and set as learning outcomes by collaborating faculty and librarians.

Databases

Databases represent traditional search systems that involve similar records and often relate to one subject or discipline. They excel at providing a sophisticated search interface that allows users to define their

Top Five Discovery Systems by One-Stop Searching

Listed Chronologically

- OCLC, WorldCat Local, 2007–
- ProQuest, Summon, 2009–
- EBSCO, EBSCO Discovery Service, 2010–
- Innovative Interfaces Inc., Encore Discovery Solution, 2010–
- Ex Libris, Primo, 2010–

Source: F. William Chickering and Sharon Q. Yang, "Evaluation and Comparison of Discovery Tools: An Update," *Information Technology and Libraries* 33, no. 2 (2014): 27, Professional Development Collection, EBSCOhost, http://dx.doi.org/10.6017/ital.v33i2.3471.

A discovery service may include:

- library catalog records
- indexes and databases
- open-access content
- institutional repository records
- local digital collections
- library research guides
- library web pages

Database Vendors

ABC-CLIO
www.abc-clio.com

Alexander Street
http://alexanderstreet.com

Cambridge University Press
www.cambridge.org

EBSCOhost
https://www.ebscohost.com

Elsevier
www.elsevier.com

Engineering Village
www.engineeringvillage.com

Gale Cengage
www.cengage.com

LexisNexis
www.lexisnexis.com/en-us/gateway.page

Oxford University Press
http://global.oup.com/?cc=us

ProQuest
www.proquest.com

Salem Press
www.salempress.com

Thomson Reuters
http://thomsonreuters.com/en.html

Wiley
www.wiley.com/WileyCDA

---

information need accurately. A thesaurus of medical subject headings by the National Library of Medicine, used in PubMed, MEDLINE, or CINAHL, or an industry code for products such as the North American Industry Classification System, used in business databases, represent just two advanced features database searchers may employ. Databases are Boolean-based and enable advanced searchers who have thoughtfully defined their information need to locate matching items on a specific topic. This makes databases ideal for serious searchers. Databases may collect articles from journals, magazines, or trade publications; images and videos; government documents; dissertations; or books.

Having acknowledged the strengths of traditional databases, whether they are index and abstract or full-text, librarians are reexamining whether they ought to and can still afford to offer databases, especially when users are satisfied with "good enough." Library budgets are limited, and many libraries cannot afford to duplicate content, nor do they have to, now that web-scale discovery is available. Library administrators are economizing where possible and cancelling database subscriptions where they duplicate content or where usage is low. Discovery systems are disrupting the status quo in scholarly finding tools.

Search Engines

Millions of searchers rely on free search engines daily. Students turn to the market leader Google when conducting course-related research, according to studies like Project Information Literacy.[10] Professionals and faculty also rely on search engines and online tools. "Search results, news feeds, alerts and email are the way most readers see new content now. In fact, many researchers rarely 'read' entire journals anymore; even the concept of 'read a journal' tends to mean 'read the email TOC'!" says John Sack of HighWire Press.[11] Some researchers think library discovery channels are limited. "It is no longer enough to make sure that content is discoverable through academic channels (such as abstracting and indexing services or library platforms); we also need to consider the implications of discovery through traditional and social media platforms," says Charlie Rapple of Kuduos.[12] Publishers are supplying article metadata to vendors of index and abstract databases, as well as search engine vendors, to index article information at publishers' websites. Publishers are also

Most Popular Search Engines, August 2015

Alhea
http://us.alhea.com

AOL
http://search.aol.com/aol/webhome

Ask
www.ask.com

Bing
https://www.bing.com

Contenko
www.contenko.com

Dogpile
www.dogpile.com

DuckDuckGo
https://duckduckgo.com

Google
https://www.google.com

Info
www.info.com

InfoSpace
http://infospace.com

MyWebSearch
http://home.mywebsearch.com/index.jhtml

WebCrawler
https://www.webcrawler.com

WolframAlpha
www.wolframalpha.com

Wow
www.wow.com

Yahoo
https://www.yahoo.com

Source: eBizMBA, "The 15 Most Popular Search Engines | August 2015," www.ebizmba.com/articles/search-engines.

Portals

Digital Public Library of America
http://dp.la

Google Scholar
https://scholar.google.com

Library of Congress
https://www.loc.gov

Multnomah County Library Homework Center
https://multcolib.org/homework-center

Public Library of Science
https://www.plos.org

Social Work Portal
www.socialworkers.org/swportal

USA.gov
https://www.usa.gov

Virtual Religion Index
http://virtualreligion.net/vri/index.html

---

working with Google Scholar and send Google Scholar information so its search engine locates article PDF links for subscribers and open-access materials.[13]

Independent searchers turn to search engines for quick, convenient access to information. They value the Semantic Web and linked data to an institution's library holdings. "Companies such as Google and Microsoft offer comprehensive search services to users free with advertisements and sponsored links, the only reminder that these are commercial enterprises."[14] Open search systems provide a free alternative to commercial search products that searchers find attractive. Cost-minded library administrators are considering how and where to spend their limited budgets. It is no longer possible to assume that students and faculty will necessarily choose an academic library's expensive and varied finding tools.

Portals

Portals are gateways to related websites on the Internet and are built by people with subject expertise applying selection standards. Beginning a search at a portal, rather than a search engine that automatically applies algorithms, leads the researcher to quality information faster. If a student needs US federal government information, then going to USA.gov makes sense because this is the official portal for US agencies and departments. If a student wants librarian-vetted websites for homework assignments, he could start at the Multnomah Public Library Homework Center. If a scholar wants notable websites, then Google Scholar, which links to the library holdings of her university library, is a fine choice. There are many discipline-specific portals, such as the Virtual Religion Network for religion websites, the Social Work Portal, or the Public Library of Science for open-access articles in science.

Notes

1. F. William Chickering and Sharon Q. Yang, "Evaluation and Comparison of Discovery Tools: An Update," *Information Technology and Libraries* 33, no. 2: 5, Professional Development Collection, EBSCOhost, http://ejournals.bc.edu/ojs/index.php/ital/article/view/3471/pdf_1.
2. Jeff Wisniewski, "Beyond the Single Search Box:

Discovery Systems," Control-Shift, *Online Searcher* 38, no. 2 (March/April 2014): 75, CINAHL Plus with Full Text, EBSCOhost.
3. Chickering and Yang, "Evaluation and Comparison of Discovery Tools," 28.
4. Marshall Breeding, *The Future of Library Resource Discovery: A White Paper Commissioned by the NISO Discovery to Delivery D2D Topic Commission* (Baltimore, MD: National Information Standards Organization, February 2015), 15, www.niso.org/apps/group_public/download.php/14487/future_library_resource_discovery.pdf.
5. Tamar Sadeh, "From Search to Discovery," *Bibliothek Forschung Und Praxis* 39, no. 2 (June 2015): 214, Library, Information Science & Technology Abstracts with Full Text, EBSCOhost, http://dx.doi.org/10.1515/bfp-2015-0028.
6. Andrew D. Asher, "Search Epistemology: Teaching Students about Information Discovery," in *Not Just Where to Click: Teaching Students How to Think About Information*, Publications in Librarianship no. 68, edited by Troy A. Swanson and Heather Jagman (Chicago: American Library Association, 2015), 144.
7. Ibid., 147.
8. William B. Badke, "Expertise and Authority in an Age of Crowdsourcing," in *Not Just Where to Click: Teaching Students How to Think About Information*, Publications in Librarianship no. 68, edited by Troy A. Swanson and Heather Jagman (Chicago: American Library Association, 2015), 205.
9. Ibid., 199.
10. University of Washington, Information School, Project Information Literacy, http://projectinfolit.org.
11. John Sack, quoted in "Scholarly Searching," *Research Information* no. 78 (June/July 2015): 30, Risk Management Reference Center, EBSCOhost.
12. Charlie Rapple, quoted in ibid.
13. Laird Barrett, quoted in ibid., 31.
14. Adrian O'Riordan, 2014, "Open Search Environments: The Free Alternative to Commercial Search Services," *Information Technology and Libraries* 33, no. 2 (2014): 45, Professional Development Collection, EBSCOhost, http://dx.doi.org/10.6017/ital.v33i2.4520.

Chapter 4

Choosing Content-Creation Products

The LMS Embedded Librarian as a Content Creator

Once librarians enter the learning management system (LMS) and become involved in individual courses, they are able to create and embed learning materials that students can use. The prior chapters examined the content that libraries provide (articles, e-books, data, etc.) and the finding tools that researchers use; this chapter will cover products and methods for communicating the value of these items and identifying how to use them to their fullest. This is where the embedded librarian can use the platform of the LMS and her presence in the course to easily share chosen resources and to directly teach students. The expectation that students will turn to the LMS to learn about their assignments and look for guidance in completing them creates a teachable moment for librarians.

Librarians can create many types of instructional objects and collections of resources to include in a course site. Course guides or subject guides can be utilized to list links of fitting resources for a course. These guides can be created for a specific embedded course, or a librarian can utilize guides that were linked on the library website for students conducting research in a topic area. Online presentations can be created to help students work through the process of planning their research or learn the important elements of citing sources or using a particular database. Screencasts often take a similar approach to that of a linear presentation, perhaps even including some slides or images created for a presentation and adding video of searching for articles or moving around on a website to make the guidance easier to understand in context. Interactive tutorials or games can be created to teach information literacy skills by, for example, asking users to decide which sources are the best to use in a particular case or to try their hands at evaluating sources. Whether it covers a broad search strategy for assignment-focused information, lists key databases, or shares the essential details of navigating a finding tool, creating custom content for a course is key for librarians in sharing library resources in the LMS.

Course and Subject Guides

The LMS lends itself to easily posting documents of several kinds. A librarian could compose a list of database URLs and other helpful text in word processing software, save it as a PDF file, and post it in the course site. It is just as easy to compose a document in the LMS's content editor (or HTML editor if you are comfortable working with HTML) and offer that page to students in the course. Pretty much any method you have for creating a list of resources for students to read over and click on will work in your LMS. But many librarians are using products outside of the LMS to accomplish this purpose. One reason is that course or subject guides are useful ways to communicate relevant resources not just to students in a specific LMS course, but also to students who are taking similar courses or studying a related subject. Librarians can create a guide that will work in multiple venues and can save time by building the guide only once. The guides can have a common style that makes them more recognizable as being associated with the library or parent institution, and a common format also makes it easier for students to learn how to navigate the guide. The guide can be linked on the library's website, embedded in the LMS for one or more courses, and shared by URL in e-mails, in chat

> **Course and Subject Guide Tools**
>
> LibGuides
> http://springshare.com/libguides
>
> Smore
> http://smore.com
>
> Google Sites
> http://sites.google.com
>
> WordPress
> http://wordpress.org

> **Presentation Tools**
>
> Google Slides
> https://www.google.com/slides/about/
>
> Microsoft PowerPoint
> https://products.office.com/en-us/powerpoint
>
> Prezi
> http://prezi.com

sessions, and on library instruction handouts for individual users or groups.

A method that has been used in a number of larger academic institutions is the automated loading of course or subject guides into LMS course sites. This is a great way to get library resources into every course that uses the LMS (and that is likely a growing percentage of all courses offered at an institution, given the statistics shared in chapter 1). This plan works, however, only if librarians at an institution have created enough guides to match the courses offered at the institution. This can be done by creating a set of guides that match all of the departments represented in the curriculum or by creating a larger, more specific set of guides for subject areas within the larger disciplines or even for each individual course. Generally, a university library might have some mixture of large subject and specific course guides to connect with course sites and then also create a general purpose research guide that can be used in courses that lack a more tailored guide. Working with the folks who administer the LMS, links or widgets can be included that will lead students from the course site back to the full course or subject guide, or perhaps the entire guide will be embedded on the course site.

LibGuides from Springshare are a popular method of providing course- or subject-related guides to library resources. Guides can be created and categorized for broad subject coverage, specific topics, individual courses, or other purposes.[1] The guides may include both links to online resources and call numbers for print materials and content may include either bulleted lists of links or segments of explanatory text. The creation of individual guides in this product is supplemented by the presentation of all of the guides in a categorized, searchable list. The process is a great mixture of flexibility in creation choices—adding different widgets, search boxes, and so forth—with the ease of standardization of layouts and overall look.

Alternative approaches to creating course and subject guides lack the organizational options built into the LibGuides system. There are easy web document creation services available like Smore.com, Google Sites, or WordPress.[2] Librarians could also code their own guides in HTML on their library websites. All of these options require the creation of style guides and templates to keep the same look and features in the guides; this process generally might require content editors to know how to create and edit HTML documents and to regularly update them. Master lists of guides also need to be updated by hand to accurately reflect changes in the names of guides, to add new guides, or to remove deleted guides. In some environments, staff availability and expertise could keep these alternative approaches running flawlessly. For others, having the structure of LibGuides in place will be extremely helpful.

Presentations

The embedded librarian needs to provide guidance to students on finding information for their projects in addition to providing links to the resources that students will use. The course guide approach can allow for the entry of brief notes or suggestions on search strategies or choosing among databases, but for a more extended introduction, a librarian may wish to link to a presentation in the LMS or on the course guide. Online presentation options allow for a generally linear presentation of informative content, giving students a way to learn about information sources, database searching, navigation skills, and related information literacy skills. The presentation can, to some degree, replace elements of a face-to-face library instruction session in that an effective presentation can identify key terms and elements for students to understand and put the use of different library resources into context.

Along with the options mentioned below, there is also the possibility of including images, audio, video, and hyperlinks to resources within the presentation. There is quite a bit of crossover among the tools mentioned in this chapter, where a presentation might include a link to a screencast, or a screencast might include introductory slides created in a presentation, and so forth. There are a wide variety of free and licensed products available for creating presentations to share with students. Some commonly available ones are listed in the gray box, including the licensed Microsoft PowerPoint and the free Google Slides and

> **Screencast Tools**
>
> Adobe Captivate
> www.adobe.com/products/captivate.html
>
> TechSmith Camtasia
> https://www.techsmith.com/camtasia.html
>
> Articulate Storyline
> https://www.articulate.com/products/storyline-why.php
>
> TechSmith Jing
> www.techsmith.com/jing.html
>
> Screencast-O-Matic
> http://screencast-o-matic.com

> **Interactive Tutorial Tools**
>
> Guide on the Side
> http://code.library.arizona.edu/gots
>
> HapYak
> http://corp.hapyak.com
>
> Office Mix
> https://mix.office.com
>
> Twine
> http://twinery.org
>
> Zaption
> https://www.zaption.com

Prezi. Slides and Prezi are both web-based tools, while PowerPoint can be web-based through Office Online or may be installed as software on a computer or mobile device.

Screencasts

Screencasts allow audio narration over anything that can be captured on a computer display. This might include still images or individual slides from a presentation, but more commonly includes video of searching a library catalog or other resource. Screencasts can provide step-by-step guidance on the use of a database or demonstrate how to locate various resources on the library website or within the embedded librarian resources in the LMS course site. They are very effective because they show the user just how to get from the point of watching the screencast into the desired resource. In fact, a user can search a database in one browser tab or window and watch a related screencast in another.

Several software applications and online tools are available for creating screencasts.[3] The first three tools listed in the gray box are all licensed products, while the other two are free web-based options (with low-cost pro versions). Captivate, Camtasia, and Storyline all allow a user to add quizzes, video files, and other media along with screen-captured action, which makes them better for multiple types of projects, from short screencasts to lengthier videos or interactive tutorials. Screencast-O-Matic and Jing will do an excellent job of capturing screen activity and combining it with narration for an effective learning object.

Interactive Tutorials

Interactive tutorials take screencasts and presentations a step further by allowing students to not only passively read and watch information on screen, but also make choices and be assessed as they learn about research or other tasks. Tutorials can take many forms and can be created with combinations of approaches. As mentioned above, the licensed software listed in the section on screencasts could be used for a multistep tutorial that combined sections of screencasts with text instructions and quizzes, all laid out in a linear pattern or a user-chosen route through several modules. This is not to say that every interactive tutorial is a lengthy experience or filled with excessive depth on the topics addressed. The key element of these tutorials is interaction, where the user of the tutorial is asked to make a choice or give input in some way. It could involve someone watching a two-minute screencast and then answering two multiple-choice questions to help reinforce the learning. It could also be set up as a game-like trip through the research process jungle, with several choices and junctures connecting sections that cover topic development, the use of reference sources, or article searching. A key element of this experience is that it can provide students with immediate feedback on their learning.[4]

In addition to the screencasting software mentioned already, there are other approaches a librarian could use to create an interactive tutorial. You could start relatively small by adding questions for students to answer at points within a screencast or presentation. The free tools HapYak and Zaption can be used to take an existing video or screencast and add multiple-choice or open-entry questions for users to answer before moving on with the video. You could use Office Mix—a free add-on for PowerPoint—to place polls, quizzes, voice, and video into presentations and save them in a format that will work on devices whether or not they have PowerPoint installed. The open software Guide on the Side works for placing a sidebar next to a live web browser window. Users complete tasks on an actual library website or in a database as directed by the instructions in the sidebar and answer review questions that also appear there. A final tool to try is Twine, which guides you in developing a nonlinear tutorial in which students choose their own path through a series of individual pages or modules, which can be text-and-image-based or include videos. The interaction in these tools can really help students understand the material offered in the instructional object and serve as a motivator for students to continue with the tutorial.[5]

Collections of Instructional Content

Keep in mind that you do not necessarily have to create all learning objects on your own. It is true that at times you will have specific routes to databases or resources that will be made clearer if you can show how to get to the resources from your library website. And great value is added by describing or outlining a search strategy for a specific assignment with expertise gained from working with a specific instructor and the identical assignment requirements that students are facing. But sometimes others have created wonderful introductions to topics or databases that will serve your students quite well, without you having to create your own. A screencast of a navigational guide to a database will show an interface that looks much the same once the user leaves your website. It is wise to create your overall presence in the course with a mixture of self-created and shared resources.

A number of learning object collections are available that may have useful materials to use in your embedded librarian setting. One, Atomic Learning, is a commercial product composed of short videos and longer tutorial collections that introduce users to a variety of technologies and related tasks. The LibGuide Community site is made available by Springshare but may be freely searched without the requirement of subscribing to LibGuides. The others listed in the gray box are collections of learning objects created by librarians or faculty members and intended to be widely shared. YouTube is not precisely focused on learning objects, but it is a widely used channel for providing access to library screencasts and video tutorials. Searching these collections can provide helpful models on which to base your own learning objects, as well as materials you can place (with attribution) in your embedded courses.

Best Practices for Building Instructional Guides, Presentations, and Tutorials

Whenever you venture into online content creation, it is key to consider aspects or characteristics of successful content that influence your creations. Some

---

Collections of Library Instructional Content

ANTS (ANimated Tutorial Sharing) Project
www.screencast.com/users/ANTS

Atomic Learning (Higher Education)
https://www.atomiclearning.com/highed

LibGuides Community (search for created LibGuides by keyword)
http://libguides.com

MERLOT (Multimedia Educational Resource for Learning and Online Teaching; look under Academic Support Services and then the Library and Information Services category)
www.merlot.org

PRIMO (Peer-Reviewed Instructional Materials Online) Database
http://primodb.org

YouTube (search for a database name or library skill topic)
https://www.youtube.com

---

practices to consider when creating content include the following:

- **Simplify.** Be careful about the length of videos or the amount of text you are expecting students to watch or read. Stick to the essentials you need to share on the topic, knowing that user behavior and just-in-time information needs tend toward a more concise approach.
- **Do not trap your users.** We should simplify things as much as possible, but there are times when topics will take more than a paragraph of text or two minutes of video. Find ways in your creations for users to skip past what they already know to learn what they do not. Modularize what you are presenting so that they can jump ahead or pick out just the video about one aspect of, say, citing articles from a particular database.
- **Watch your language.** Think about your audience, where they are coming from, and what level of understanding they have. Avoid library lingo, except where it is useful for users to learn it. Try to phrase what you have to say in active ways.
- **Context is king.** Make sure that you are including fitting information in your learning object that does not go off on tangents. The learning object should stay focused on the information need you are trying to address so that users stick with it and see its value.
- **Seek interaction and application.** Help users learn the material by having a ready chance to

apply their knowledge. This might be through an interactive addition to a presentation or video, or it might be a case of providing learning objects when students are preparing or working on an assignment connected to library resources.[6]

Keeping these practices in mind, it is key for embedded librarians to put their best feet forward with the students and faculty they are trying to serve. Make content that fits the courses you are working with. Find content that will meet needs and save you time by eliminating repeated effort. Share content with your users and make an impact on their searching skills and choices.

Notes

1. Ruth L. Baker, "Designing LibGuides as Instructional Tools for Critical Thinking and Effective Online Learning," *Journal of Library and Information Services in Distance Learning* 8, no. 3–4 (2014): 107–17.
2. See, as an example of a library guide created with Smore.com, "Research Resources," Villa Maria College, accessed October 28, 2015, www.villa.edu/academics/library/research-resources.
3. Christine Forbes, "Free Web-Based Tools for Information Literacy Instruction," *Library Hi Tech News* 31, no. 10 (2014): 1–5.
4. Katie Greer, Amanda Nichols Hess, and Elizabeth W. Kraemer, "The Librarian Leading the Machine: A Reassessment of Library Instruction Methods," *College and Research Libraries* preprint, accepted April 2015, anticipated publication date May 1, 2016, http://crl.acrl.org/content/early/2015/05/11/crl15-719.full.pdf+html.
5. Mandi Goodsett, "Creating Interactive Tutorials Using Free Resources: Home," Cleveland State University, Michael Schwartz Library, 2015, http://researchguides.csuohio.edu/interactivetutorials.
6. Janice (Ginny) Redish, *Letting Go of the Words: Writing Web Content That Works*, (San Francisco: Morgan Kaufmann, 2007).

Chapter 5

Communicating, Collaboration, and Citing

LMS Embedded Librarianship

Creating a virtual presence, online collaboration, and academic integrity are hallmarks of LMS embedded librarianship. Embedded librarianship necessitates communication and collaboration with faculty who open their LMS courses and with their enrolled students. Online communication and collaboration become all the more important when the embedded librarian works only virtually with stakeholders in the LMS environment due to geographic distance or scheduling conflicts. To be effective as an online research consultant, the LMS embedded librarian relies on a variety of communication tools to fulfill tasks: to identify the faculty member's research assignment learning outcomes and propose relevant research strategies, library resources, and services. Sometimes these conversations lead to assignment redesign or the creation of new tutorials and guides. LMS embedded librarians proactively engage student researchers and respond as called upon by individuals to confer on information literacy challenges throughout the research process. Some hold virtual office hours to meet and consult with students. Others hold synchronous help sessions that are recorded and shared with students who could not otherwise attend. Sometimes chat or e-mail suffices as a communication method. Librarians intentionally build trusted relationships with individual students in order to share their bibliographic and technology expertise. Often embedded librarians carefully select and share tested online collaboration tools that students may use to complete their group research projects and presentations. In addition, academic research requires adhering to academic integrity protocols, the chief one being source citation in a discipline's accepted style.

Thankfully, there are many citation generators and managers available today that simplify citing sources. These citation tools, guides, and tutorials are typically included on the embedded librarian's page and sent to students in other messages. In all these ways, embedded librarians reach out to communicate, collaborate, and teach information literacy within a LMS course.

Communicating with Students

E-mail, which has been in use for fifty years, has replaced physical and voice mail as the primary communication method in academe, business, and government. It is flexible and efficient in that information and messages can be exchanged asynchronously. The ability to attach articles, scanned documents, presentations, and images maximizes the usefulness of the brief e-mail. E-mail has expanded to mobile platforms like smartphones and tablet computers. E-mail service providers like Google, Microsoft, and Yahoo! provide e-mail hosting servers and compete for customers by offering features related to their other product lines. Some paid e-mail services like Microsoft rely on downloaded software and are typically used by large organizations, hosted on their own e-mail hosting servers and equipment. Other, free e-mail services like Gmail rely on web browsers and cloud computing. E-mail has become a low-cost marketing tool, used to reach potential customers or, in academe, to reach students. Spam, unsolicited commercial e-mail filling one's inbox, and attachments that carry computer viruses are two problems associated with e-mail. Spam filters and computer security industries arose to combat these problems and are an added expense for organizations using e-mail. Google and Microsoft are

Free E-mail

Google Gmail
https://mail.google.com/mail

Paid E-mail

Microsoft Outlook
www.microsoft.com/en-us/outlook-com

Chat/IM

LibraryH3lp (Paid)
https://us.libraryh3lp.com

OCLC QuestionPoint (Paid)
www.questionpoint.org

Zopim (1 agent only Free)
https://www.zopim.com

---

the leading e-mail service providers and offer a wide range of features.

Faculty and embedded librarians communicate with students regularly to announce, remind, explain, encourage, and update students about upcoming course details and changes. Often instructors choose to mass e-mail all or selected registered students using the LMS course e-mail. At other times, instructors will opt to post and e-mail an announcement so that students receive a personal message in their inbox and also see the message posted as an announcement in the LMS course. The LMS e-mail tool saves time and makes ongoing communication easier. LMS embedded librarians assigned to specific courses also have the means to mass e-mail an entire class in regard to research assignments and to offer strategies and links to electronic resources. Virtual reference services inside the LMS and also based in the library utilize e-mail in addition to text, chat, and web conferencing.

LMS Collaboration Tools

Connectivism is a pedagogical method employing collaboration. "Connectivism focuses on learning that occurs when individuals interact socially using collaborative technologies. The connectivist learner produces knowledge through creating and sharing digital artifacts."[1] LMS collaboration tools improve communication, learning, and teaching among students and between student and instructor. Most LMSs include various collaboration tools such as blogs, wikis, discussions, and groups. Each has its purpose. For added sensory input there are collaborative tools that permit inserting images and recording audio podcasts and videos. Collaborative tools in different LMSs may have somewhat different names, such as forums, discussions, or discussion boards. These collaborative tools may function more or less effectively, from LMS to LMS, based on user and reviewer feedback. The intent of collaborative tools is to allow users to interact, build community, and strengthen collaboration. "Many of the underused LMS features (e.g., those that involve collaboration) have the potential to enhance student learning and engagement."[2]

Sometimes these lofty goals are not reached, however, due either to pedagogical methods employed or to technology obstacles. According to an EDUCAUSE report, the LMS collaborative tools are the least liked. "Today, user satisfaction is highest for basic LMS features and lowest for features designed to foster collaboration and engagement."[3] Although students are using mobile devices more to access LMS course content, their use of educational technologies has remained steady over the past five years. Students admit wanting more peer collaboration technologies; however, "this study reveals a noticeable increase in the demand for more online technologies for assessment, collaboration with peers, administrative purposes and access to resources such as podcasts, lecture recordings and online library resources."[4]

As mentioned above, LMS collaboration tools include blogs, wikis, discussions, and groups.

- **Blogs** are online journals created by individuals or groups to share activities, information, news, opinions, or research. They may include text, hyperlinks, images, audio, and video and solicit comments by others. Blogs build community and allow for collective reflection.
- **Wikis** can be used to organize information by numerous contributors on this "quick" website. Wikis promote interaction and cooperation through shared creation.
- **Discussions** are sometimes called discussion boards or forums. Students respond to the instructor's prompt and often comment on one another's posts, thus mirroring a face-to-face classroom discussion or conversation.
- Instructors often assign students to **groups** within the LMS. Then students work together on projects, presentations, and papers by using those LMS tools that enable groups to chat, e-mail, and share documents and files.

In addition to LMS collaboration tools, there are many third-party vendor products and free sites that offer tools for student collaborations and group work in connection with study and research, teaching and learning, or presenting and publishing. Outside the LMS, instructors may use third-party products that rely on cloud computing and include single sign-on, APIs, and dashboards for sharing data across

Blog Software

Ghost (Paid)
https://ghost.org

LinkedIn (Free)
https://www.linkedin.com

Postach.io (Evernote, Free)
http://postach.io/site

Silvrback (Paid)
https://www.silvrback.com

TinyPress (Github, Free)
https://tinypress.co

Tumblr (Free)
https://www.tumblr.com

Weebly (Free)
www.weebly.com

WordPress (Free)
https://wordpress.com

Hosted Wiki Software

DokuWiki (Free)
https://www.dokuwiki.org/dokuwiki#

EditMe (Paid)
www.editme.com

PBworks (Free)
www.pbworks.com

SharePoint (Paid)
https://products.office.com/en-us/sharepoint/collaboration

Wikispaces Classroom (Free)
https://www.wikispaces.com/content/classroom

WikiSpaces Campus (Paid)
https://www.wikispaces.com

Wikis Needing Web Hosting Provider

Drupal
https://www.drupal.org

Tiki Wiki
https://info.tiki.org

For More Information

WikiMatrix
www.wikimatrix.org

programs.[5] Integration of LMS and cloud computing or cloud services promotes cost-effective, innovative solutions in peer collaboration.

Web Conferencing

Web conferencing offers instructional flexibility for faculty and students who cannot meet at the same time and place for classroom instruction, group work, or consultations. Web conferencing saves travel time and expense by enabling students to meet virtually with peers, librarians, faculty, or academic advisors. Anyone with a computer, webcam, Internet access, and web conferencing app or program may either teach virtually or receive course instruction as a student via video, audio, and virtual collaboration using whiteboards and group chat rooms. Sometimes instruction will be synchronous, while at other times recorded content can be accessed asynchronously when convenient for students who live at a distance, who have competing job or family responsibilities, or who have disabilities that complicate travel.

Universities employ web conferencing solutions for different scenarios. Sometimes universities with multiple campuses offer a traditional course on one campus and register students from its other branch campuses who attend virtually via WebEx, Interactive Video Distance Learning (IVDL), and so on. This blended synchronous learning maximizes the instructional reach of a university's faculty by enrolling students who typically take courses on other campuses. Web conferencing is essential for distance education for both web and hybrid courses. Web conferencing also strengthens teaching and learning in traditional courses as the instructor may hold virtual office hours, provide recorded course content reviews, or flip the classroom, which involves students listening to recorded lectures, demonstrations, and presentations outside class. Classroom time is then reserved for problem solving, discussions, and experiential learning that emphasizes interactive, engaged activities.

Web conferencing enlarges the reach of universities that exclusively offer online courses as well as established institutions that desire to expand course offerings virtually. "Through William & Mary's virtual learning world, students can listen to pre-recorded lectures, attend live interactive sessions led by the professors and engage with other students in small group projects. Professors hold weekly office hours in AvayaLive Engage that provide the personal connection and help eliminate many scheduling issues tied to time and place."[6]

There are numerous web conferencing software programs available, some proprietary and others free. Blackboard Collaborate offers typical features:

> Blackboard Collaborate is a web-based collaboration platform that is available through Blackboard, Inc. (Blackboard Collaborate, n.d.). It offers the capabilities of hosting real-time sessions, has a whiteboard feature, allows desktop sharing, and

Web Conferencing Platforms

Adobe Connect (Paid)
www.adobe.com/products/adobeconnect.html

AvayaLive Engage (Paid)
https://engage.avayalive.com/Engage

Blackboard Collaborate (Paid)
www.blackboard.com/online-collaborative-learning/index.aspx

Cisco WebEx (Free for 3 otherwise Paid)
www.webex.com

FaceTime for Mac (Free)
www.apple.com/mac/facetime

Google Hangouts (Free)
https://hangouts.google.com

Join.Me (Free)
https://www.join.me

Onstream (Free)
www.onstreammedia.com

Skype (Free)
www.skype.com/en

Free Document Sharing

Bitrix24
https://www.bitrix24.com

Google Docs
https://www.google.com/docs/about

Jumpshare
https://jumpshare.com

Microsoft Office 365
https://products.office.com/en-US/student/office-in-education

Zoho Docs
https://www.zoho.com/docs

Cloud Storage Solutions

Amazon Cloud Drive (Paid)
https://www.amazon.com/clouddrive/home

Apple iCloud (Free)
https://www.icloud.com

Box (Paid)
https://www.box.com

Copy (Paid)
https://www.copy.com/page/home;section:landing

Dropbox (Free)
https://www.dropbox.com/en

Google Drive (Free)
https://www.google.com/drive

Mega (Free)
https://mega.nz/#

Microsoft OneDrive (Free)
https://onedrive.live.com/about/en-us

SugarSync (Paid)
https://www.sugarsync.com

Wikipedia: Comparison of file hosting services
https://en.wikipedia.org/wiki/Comparison_of_file_hosting_services

---

is an engagement as well as a communication tool. The software has video, audio, and phone conferencing capabilities, as well as a chat feature. Collaborate sessions can be recorded and the link to a recorded session can be emailed out to students or posted as podcasts on iTunes or other web-based sites.[7]

Web conferencing applications such as Skype and Adobe Connect enable Australian universities to utilize effective synchronous and asynchronous sessions to supervise teaching practicums, where the university professor, supervising teacher, and trainee student-teacher may meet without the need for travel.[8]

Faculty assign students to research, write, present, and problem solve as a group. Students today work in collaborative learning environments as team members as they will in the workforce. They typically employ productivity tools to collaborate electronically. It does not matter whether they live on the same campus, in the same city, or in different time zones. Students may create technology projects, write papers, build presentations, and analyze cases in groups. They share drafts of text, spreadsheets, slides, surveys, podcasts, video tutorials, code, and so on. Each student contributes his portion to the larger group. Collaborative learning necessitates access to shared documents and spaces. Cloud computing has become the most affordable and convenient solution because data is stored on remote servers that can be accessed anytime from anywhere. Those invited to access, view, and edit these shared documents can start the project on campus and continue working on the current version at home.

Commonly students use Google Drive to share documents, sheets, slides, and forms because it is free. Zoho is another popular, free productivity tool. Sometimes proprietary products like Office 365 are used to share work.

Large files and documents can be saved and retrieved from shared spaces using installed software and apps. Once Dropbox is installed on one's computers and mobile computing devices, it can be used to save and retrieve files as needed.

Free Citation Generators

BibMe
www.bibme.org

EasyBib
www.easybib.com

Citefast
www.citefast.com

Cite This For Me
https://www.citethisforme.com

GoBiblio
http://gobiblio.com

Landmark, Son of Citation Machine
www.citationmachine.net

NoodleTools Express
www.noodletools.com/noodlebib/express.php

OttoBib
www.ottobib.com

Free Reference Managers

Mendeley
https://www.mendeley.com

Qiqqa
www.qiqqa.com

RefME
https://www.refme.com/i/b

Zotero
https://www.zotero.org

Paid Reference Managers

RefWorks
https://www.refworks.com

EndNote
http://endnote.com

Wikipedia: Comparison of reference management software
https://en.wikipedia.org/wiki/Comparison_of_reference_management_software

Citation Tools

Citing sources is an essential practice in research and signals adherence to academic integrity. Embedded librarians regularly provide information literacy instruction on citing sources, often at the request of instructors. Today, citation tools, featuring many style formats, are built into proprietary databases, library discovery services, and search engines like Google Scholar. Experienced researchers take advantage of these efficient, convenient tools to cite sources as they search for needed information.

The chosen citation style often depends on the subject discipline. Generally Modern Language Association style is used in the humanities while American Psychological Association style is used in the social sciences. Chicago or Turabian style is used in history. The sciences use a variety of styles: National Library of Medicine style in biology, American Chemical Society style in chemistry, American Society of Civil Engineers style for civil engineering, Institute of Electrical and Electronics Engineers for those engineering subsets, LaTex for mathematics and statistics. For more information, see the "Complete Discipline Listing" at Purdue University's Online Writing Lab.

Complete Discipline Listing, Online Writing Lab, Purdue University
https://owl.english.purdue.edu/owl/resource/585/2

Beyond the finding tools themselves, students may avail themselves of citation generators and citation managers to get help citing sources. Often students who need to cite only several sources will turn to citation generators to produce automatically a correct citation for that source type, in a specific citation style. There are both free and proprietary citation generators available online. Many college and university libraries build their own citation generators, such as CitationBuilder by North Carolina State University Libraries or KnightCite by Calvin College Library. Online citation generators may be partially free for certain citation styles, charge users for other citation styles; accept ads so that users are not charged, or they may be entirely free.

Reference managers are intended to provide more bibliographic, sophisticated functions. They are used to store many source citations and create extensive bibliographies in a wide array of styles as needed.

Notes

1. Neena Thota and Joao G. M. Negreiros, "Introducing Educational Technologies to Teachers: Experience Report," *Journal of University Teaching and Learning Practice* 12, no. 1 (2015): 2, Education Research Complete, EBSCOhost.
2. Eden Dahlstrom, D. Christopher Brooks, and Jacqueline Bichsel, *The Current Ecosystem of Learning Management Systems in Higher Education: Student, Faculty, and IT Perspectives,* research report (Louisville, CO: EDUCAUSE Center for Analysis and Research, September 2014), 4, https://net.educause.edu/ir/library/pdf/ers1414.pdf.
3. Ibid., 23.
4. Negin Mirriahi and Dennis Alonzo, "Shedding Light

on Students' Technology Preferences: Implications for Academic Development," *Journal of University Teaching and Learning Practice* 12, no. 1 (2015): 11, Education Research Complete, EBSCOhost.
5. Dian Schaffhauser, "10 Tech Tools That Inspire PBL in High School," *T H E Journal* 41, no. 5 (May 2014): 10, MasterFILE Premier, EBSCOhost.
6. Avaya, "Avaya Helps Higher Education Institutions Create Innovative Learning Environments for Greater Student Engagement," news release, September 29, 2014, Points of View Reference Center, EBSCOhost, www.avaya.com/usa/about-avaya/newsroom/news-releases/2014/pr-140929.
7. Stephanie J. Jones and Kinsey Hansen, "Technology Review: Virtual Intrusive Advising—Supporting Community College Students through Web-Based Synchronous Technologies," *Community College Enterprise* 20, no. 1 (2014): 91, Education Research Complete, EBSCOhost.
8. Yiong Hwee Teo, Sue McNamara, Geoff Romeo, and Donna Gronn, "Enhancing Practicum Supervision with Asynchronous and Synchronous Technologies," *Universal Journal of Educational Research* 3, no. 5 (2015): 322–27, ERIC, EBSCOhost.

Chapter 6

Universal Design and Copyright Considerations

The Impacts of Universal Design and Copyright on LMS Embedded Librarianship

The goals of embedded librarians can be expressed in many different ways, given the varieties of courses they work with and the differing needs of individual students and priorities of individual faculty. However, key on the mind of every embedded librarian is the need to have the materials shared in the course accessible to all students. Likewise, librarians want to make sure that information resources are used as fully as they can be while still keeping that use within the law. Both of these factors can fill us at once with a sense of opportunity and with a fear that we must follow the rules or risk disaster. These motivations should not become a legal yoke of expectations for librarians to comply with, but rather they should free us to make the most of our embedded experience for our students.

Universal Design

First of all, it is good to get a clear idea of what universal design is. The concept in short is focused on making a service or an object work well for people who have a wide range of skills and abilities.[1] For embedded librarians, this means that we need to ask if the resources we share, the instructional tools we offer, and the course site we use are truly available to everyone who is taking the course. It is a fair question to ask of existing services and also one to posit as we plan out our activities. We should think widely here about the audience for our services and consider not only whether or not students in the course may have disabilities but also imagine individuals who may not be proficient English speakers or people who may be new to using technology or library databases.[2] Given the spot where we are meeting and interacting with our students, there are many opportunities for barriers to appear.

Following Instructional Design Principles

Given the broad nature of these potential barriers, it may serve the embedded librarian well to work with a more formal set of instructional design principles. This approach can guide our development of embedded librarian pages and learning objects, making our services and operations more transparent and accessible to all of our users.

One model of instructional design goes by the acronym *ADDIE*, which stands for Analysis, Design, Development, Implementation, and Evaluation.[3] ADDIE is used widely in designing learning environments to meet their intended outcomes and to assess how well they perform.

It is useful to use the items in the acronym as steps to take (and repeat) when designing materials for the embedded librarian presence in a course. Briefly, the steps work like this. First, you analyze the background of the course and the environment you are working in: what does the instructor expect of students, what resources make the most sense to introduce, what do students already know about the subject matter, when in the course is it most fitting to introduce particular skills or resources? Then, you move to design what you will offer the course participants and when to offer it in the course: contact information for the librarian, list

> **The ADDIE Model of Instructional System Design**
> - Analysis
> - Design
> - Development
> - Implementation
> - Evaluation

> **Accessibility Design Resources**
>
> American Federation for the Blind, "Creating Accessible Websites"
> www.afb.org/info/accessibility/creating-accessible-websites/23
>
> CAST (Center for Applied Special Technology)
> www.cast.org
>
> Section 508 of the Rehabilitation Act
> www.section508.gov
>
> WebAIM (Web Accessibility in Mind)
> http://webaim.org/articles
>
> World Wide Web Consortium (W3C) Web Accessibility Initiative
> www.w3.org/WAI

of databases, screencasts or interactive tutorials, guidance on citing sources, monitoring a forum or discussion board, and so on. In the middle of the process comes development, in which you create or locate the materials you will need and prepare text you will use in the course. Then there is the implementation stage, where you actually put everything into place, allowing for adjustments along the way as you make the final fit with material the instructor has posted. Finally, you evaluate the embedded experience, both by querying students and faculty and by making self-assessments of how well the design worked.[4] And then the cycle begins anew, with the next embedded course improving on the lessons learned from each prior offering.

Accessible Design Considerations

This discussion of ADDIE leads well into considering the issue of accessibility when analyzing the environment of the course and the eventual design and development of materials to include in the embedded librarian presence. It is important to remember that there may be individuals taking part in the course with extremely low vision or no vision who are accessing these electronic resources using screen-reader software or other adaptive means. Designing online content means that you have to consider how learning objects or embedded librarian pages will display in a text-based browser or how well alt tags will convey what an image represents. Captioning, which addresses the needs of students with hearing impairments and those using text-based browsers, needs to be available for screencasts or videos as well. These are just a few of the considerations that must be made to ensure that your resources are usable. Several design standards are available that can help guide you in this design. Be sure to check the sites listed in the gray box for background reading, specific guidance, and sites that can help test out your content.

Responsive Design

One further exploration of universal design is the recognition that resources must function well on various types of devices. Mobile devices, such as tablets and smartphones, have reduced screen sizes when compared to desktop and laptop computers, and they are growing steadily in use. Embedded librarians need to consider what their learning objects and pages look like on smaller screens. Responsive design is an approach to designing websites and database interfaces so that they scale nicely between different screen sizes and resolutions. Following the tenets of responsive design can ensure that pages are adjusted to work in these situations. It is sometimes used as an alternative to building a separate mobile site or app for a site or a product like an LMS.[5]

Copyright Considerations in LMS Embedded Librarianship

While this is not an extensive examination of copyright, it seems appropriate to address some issues related to licensed resources and how they may be used in educational settings. Going back to the start of this chapter, if the embedded librarian intends to ensure access to licensed materials to the widest extent possible under the law, then we had better understand the law. Copyright law is established to protect the rights of copyright holders to profit from what they create. The fair use provision in the law allows for a variety of possible educational uses of copyrighted materials, and the TEACH Act extends some further educational uses to the digital realm. More information on each of these is available in the resources listed in the gray box, but generally, in an academic setting, in the LMS, instructors and students are operating in an environment where they can use many licensed resources without fear of challenging copyright law or overstepping the provisions of licenses.

So, what does this mean for how embedded librarians act? We can guide faculty in placing links to online

> **Copyright and Licensing Resources**
>
> Fair Use—Columbia University Libraries Copyright Advisory Office
> https://copyright.columbia.edu/basics/fair-use.html
>
> The TEACH Act and Some Frequently Asked Questions—American Library Association
> www.ala.org/advocacy/copyright/teachact/faq
>
> About—Creative Commons
> http://creativecommons.org/about

resources (articles, digital videos, e-books, etc.) in their course sites rather than posting PDFs or video files (though it can be argued that this is a proper fair use activity) since posting a link precludes making a copy of something. We can model good behavior for students by citing the items we link to or refer to in text or videos we create, giving credit where credit is due. We are not the copyright police, but rather educators and guides to copyright and licensing issues. Aufderheide and Jaszi's book is an excellent read on other ways to imagine and apply fair use and the TEACH Act, both of which have great relevance to our work in the LMS.[6]

And, in addition to licensed resources, embedded librarians can also advocate for the use of various open items that use alternative copyright measures or none at all. These may include open educational resources (OERs), which were addressed in chapter 2, or various Creative Commons–licensed works, which are made available for use and sometimes remixing and reuse so long as credit is given. We can also make use of Creative Commons–licensed materials and images in our learning objects, giving credit as required by the licenses.

Providing access, protecting and teaching the principles of access, and designing to ensure access: three excellent roles for the embedded librarian. Pursuing these aims serves our students and faculty well as we accompany them in the LMS.

Notes

1. Janet Gronneberg and Sam Johnston, *Seven Things You Should Know about Universal Design for Learning* (Louisville, CO: EDUCAUSE Learning Initiative, April 6, 2015), www.educause.edu/library/resources/7-things-you-should-know-about-universal-design-learning.
2. Lisa Felix, "Design for Everyone." *Library Journal* 133, no. 16 (2008): 38–40.
3. Steven J. Bell and John D. Shank, *Academic Librarianship by Design: A Blended Librarian's Guide to the Tools and Techniques* (Chicago: American Library Association, 2007).
4. Beth E. Tumbleson and John Burke, *Embedding Librarianship in Learning Management Systems: A How-To-Do-It Manual* (Chicago: Neal-Schuman, an imprint of the American Library Association, 2013), 70–88.
5. Nick Pettit, "The 2014 Guide to Responsive Web Design," *Team Treehouse* (blog), June 2, 2014, http://blog.teamtreehouse.com/modern-field-guide-responsive-web-design.
6. Patricia Aufderheide and Peter Jaszi, *Reclaiming Fair Use: How to Put Balance Back in Copyright* (Chicago: University of Chicago Press, 2011).

Notes

Notes

Notes

Library Technology REPORTS

	Upcoming Issues	
April 52:3	**Mobile Learning Trends: Accessibility, Ecosystems, Content Creation** by Nicole Hennig	
May/June 52:4	**Privacy in Library Automation Products** by Marshall Breeding	
July 52:5	**Improving Visibility on the Web** by Ted Fons	

Subscribe
alatechsource.org/subscribe

Purchase single copies in the ALA Store
alastore.ala.org

alatechsource.org

ALA TechSource, a unit of the publishing department of the American Library Association

www.ingramcontent.com/pod-product-compliance
Lightning Source LLC
Chambersburg PA
CBHW080925300426
44115CB00018B/2948